HOW TO WRITE
A BOOK ABOUT
WEIGHT LOSS

or any other non-fiction topic

ROBERT J BANNON

2nd edition 2024

Dedicated to all the lifelong learners who live by the motto

It's never too late

Contents

FORWARD

Writing a book about weight loss, or any other non-fiction topic, is within your grasp if you can bring expertise or personal experience to the exercise. Sure, there are lots of books out there already, but your unique perspective will resonate with many people because they share your point of view, your challenge or simply need your unique help.

This book has been created for people who want to write a NON-FICTION book and deals with the many intricacies of writing and publishing that genre.

Most early-stage authors who want to write a non-fiction book also have a full-time career or responsibilities. This book and program have been designed especially for them. If you use this book as your template and commit one hour per day to your own writing, you will complete a well-written manuscript that will bring credibility, opportunity, and perhaps much more to you. You do not need to be a professional writer, English literature major, or a graduate student of spelling, punctuation, and grammar to become a successful author. You need a reason to create a book, an opinion to share, knowledge to pass along, a perspective to offer, a story to tell, a desire for increased exposure, recognition, or credibility. It also helps, but is not essential, if you can honestly include in your various networking "profiles" the word, reader. Almost every bestselling author started out by being a habitual reader – just ask someone like Stephen King.

To be a successful author in this world, you might need some guidance, encouragement, and advice, and you now have that before your eyes. That, combined with the willingness to carve out an hour a day from your overloaded schedule, will create a new status for your profile, "published author."

INTRODUCTION

"Oh, you're writing a book. I've tried to write a book several times and can't seem to get past the first few pages. How did you do it?"

Everyone who has shared the fact that they have written a book has heard this remark from an erstwhile, yet struggling, author-in-the-making. You may have decided to read this book because you have experienced the same problem - can't get past the first few pages, can't find the time, and can't seem to get motivated. I understand what you are going through because I have heard it many times from clients or workshop attendees. Or, I have used the same excuses myself. With little planning, I powered my way through my first book by leaving a job I hated for an hour every morning. Sitting at a table in a nearby shopping mall food court, I spent the time writing. It was an escape, to be sure, but I still felt like I was accomplishing something. Justification of my daily ritual was easy. Fortunately, the routine worked so well that I wrote a second book in the same manner but created a better working process for myself. Writing allowed a creative energy to release itself that had been kindled through a strong interest in stage acting, but which had remained unfulfilled beyond high school.

An outlet for something that had been bottled up inside for several decades came forward. Along the way, I spent over thirty years in various business environments that resulted in several things, but especially a strong need to bring "process" to a project and keep a constant eye on both sales and the bottom line.

Following the publication of my first book, **The West Coast Trail: One Step at a Time**, my wife threw a big party and invited a lot of friends. Several things came to light as a result: first, I sold over a hundred books that night (it almost paid for the party) which was great. My ego took an enormous boost from all the flattering (and a few envious) comments. I cannot count how many times I heard the sentence I started this introduction with, "I've tried to write a book several times too, but..."

Now, I was surrounded that night by some very intelligent, well-spoken, motivated, and interesting people who were more than capable of doing what I had done, or so I thought. One of the other comments that I heard then and many times since was, "I just can't seem to move it forward, can't seem to find the time and motivation..." These sorts of things played around in my mind and what developed was a back-and-forth battle between my creative self and my business self. I wanted to understand on the one hand, and help on the other.

The "process" section of my brain started looking at my own methods of writing, study other successful authors and begin researching what aids and help existed for aspiring writers. My creative side began wondering about how I could best assist people who could not create their own books. By chance, an acquaintance asked if I might provide her with some one-on-one coaching in her effort to write a book. I didn't give it much thought prior to agreeing, but once I had done so, I needed to come up with a method and series of steps that would be successful.

I used my experience, combined with an organized study of the information pertaining to creating a book, took courses, studied the teachings of others, and looked for information far and wide. This research, combined with common sense and a practical need to create deadlines, offer informed help, and set up an accountability function, allowed me to bring value to my first client. This approach worked well enough to have her recommend me to some acquaintances in the U.S., another in New Zealand, and I discovered my own connections in the UK and Canada. Thus, was born a coaching business to help aspiring authors. Workshops soon followed and, from the feedback that I received, I developed a program that will have you writing your own successful book. So, personally, I could create a coaching practice, but without some incredible changes in the publishing business, it may have meant nothing.

Self-publishing and vanity publishing have moved at astonishing rates to allow almost anyone to create and sell a book unlike anything we have ever seen in history. Hooked to the power of the internet and the realization that an author can communicate directly with her audience; the sky is the limit for writers. The digital universe is being inundated with e-books, online publishers, and bookstores, which has opened up the book tap for almost anything to be "published" regardless of quality, content or value.

In some ways, the book business has become a bit like the "wild west", no rules, no standards, every man or woman for themselves and we are being flooded with both high-quality product from previous unknowns and absolute crap created purely for ego or profit, and everything in between.

I offer this book for the early-stage author, who wants to rise above the crowd of mediocrity and create a presence in the writing world that is built on professionalism and quality. If you insist on a high standard of excellence and a consistent and credible message presented in a way that best represents who you are, then you have arrived at the right place. This is more than just a series of instructions to move you forward to a completed manuscript. It is about helping you become an author that is recognized for your ability to craft a book with care.

One that will be read, valued, and enjoyed by your readers for years to come.

Chapter 1

HOW TO USE THIS BOOK

Have you read a self-help or how-to book before? Have you done like I do and countless thousands, perhaps millions of others do? Read through the book, look at the sections labeled "lessons", and say, "That looks good. I'll come back and do that later?" Some of us have gone back and maximized our value and filled in the blanks and created the list. But, I suspect the majority put the book in their bookcase and moved on to the next one that promises a better life, better health, more money, an ideal relationship. I was told recently that after most of these books are purchased, the first chapter is read and then the balance is left lying on the bookshelf for some mysterious future when there will be more time.

Each section of this book builds upon the previous section and assumes that you have completed the action requested. The most important thing you can do is read and complete the section that deals with the question, "**What's your book about?**" This will set up everything that follows, both in this book and in your writing career, for success. The lack of an answer to that question almost always dooms the efforts of any would-be author in any genre.

Chapter 2

WHAT'S YOUR BOOK ABOUT?

Writing a book differs from writing an online article or a blog - it is more permanent and is a more solid reflection of who we are as a person. This means that we need to take the entire process more seriously. Whatever we write should be something we have passion, curiosity, knowledge, and a reasonable level of expertise about. Without doubt, our readers and the world generally treat a book with much more importance and respect than the somewhat ethereal world of digital writing on blogs, social networks, and websites. The printed page holds a mysterious power and respect for its permanence, and that is exactly why you are writing a book in the first place, isn't it?

You can write a book about WEIGHT LOSS, for instance, from many angles: as a nutrition expert, health professional, fitness instructor, or someone who has successfully lost weight, <u>or not</u>, by following the advice of gurus and experts. The important thing is to have a perspective and write from that without apology because the most important criteria is, are you providing value for your readers? Another way of looking at it is this; can you offer something in your writing that will change a reader's life for the better?

You bring to your book the sum of all your training, education, life experience, research, passion, and interest, including all your successes and failures. If you consider your credentials for writing in this context, it gives you the authority and expertise to add your book to the shelf that holds other WEIGHT LOSS books.

How do you bring your knowledge base to the level of an informed observer who has something worthwhile reading? There are several ways to do this quickly and the information age provides an opportunity to pursue any interest easily from the comfort of our computer chair. Do a long tail keyword search for the topic by using phrases that will elicit specific information about weight loss. Instead of searching "weight loss," you will want to become far more focused by looking at "weight loss for people over 60" as an example. Make your search specific and define the area as minutely as possible while monitoring how many other people might also have an interest. Use the "long tail search term" approach to research on the internet for more focused information. Narrow your focus rather than widen it. A long-tailed search term is defined as a phrase of 3 or more words.

Tim Ferriss, in his book "***The 4 - Hour Work Week***," suggests that you find a list of book titles in your chosen field and read the top three. First, you will have amassed much of the current thinking on the subject and scouted out your competition, and potential collaborators, at the same time. This will also confirm that there is a market for writing on the topic. The author's blogs or websites will usually provide additional information and links to more sources and the upshot is that you have now done enough research, combined with your personal interest, to offer your own views, in your own words, in your own book, with your own voice and ideas to the world.

"If you wait to write, you're not a writer, you're a waiter."

Dan Poynter

Chapter 3

BRAINCHILD

Your book is your "brainchild." You have probably been thinking about it for a long time. But you have not started, or perhaps, like many people, you have started but could not sustain the writing process. One of the most common stories we hear from aspiring authors is that they do not have the time to fit writing into their hectic day. If only they could take six months off, rent a beach house and with no distractions (other than the sun, sand, surf, boating, barbecues, long walks, rolling waves, etc.) the book would be magically written, and official best seller status would be conferred in only a matter of a few more weeks. Get over it - you don't have the time for that, so let's deal with the time you have - NOW.

You can continue to dream and talk about it or sit down and find an hour a day, morning, noon or night, set it aside and become a monk for that short period. There is no exception to this. You and I both have an hour a day in our existing schedule and if you must stick to your story - get up an hour earlier or go to bed an hour later - your choice. It must be consistent every day. Without question, the time needs to be the same. Create the time starting to-day, even if you are not prepared to begin the actual writing process. The time can be used for working on this program, research, planning and organizing your material to get started. We will cover the time element later as we get closer to the actual writing process.

Let's be honest, you might just not know how or where to start and that is alright. If you are not a bridge engineer and decided to build one, you would not know where to start either. If writing is an unfamiliar experience for you, then it will take some effort and perhaps some help to get started, and that is what this system is all about. In addition, your book concept may be unclear. Knowing you have a book inside you is one thing, but knowing what that book is all about and translating what is probably a bunch of disjointed thoughts into a completed manuscript requires some new skills. Give yourself a break here and now. We will start from start and move you through the process in an organized and comfortable fashion. You will complete your book, but first you must give yourself the space and time in your head to accomplish it.

It is amazing how much energy it takes to hold on to a creative idea and until now; you have had no outlet to help you move forward. Just a quick tip here: start carrying a notebook and pen and jot down those random thoughts and phrases as soon as they occur to you. It will take the pressure off trying to remember an idea for your book. This is incredibly important and is a practice you have probably already thought about, anyway. Start this moment.

There is always some guilt around knowing you should write a book and then not taking any action in that direction - "I know I should, I know I should..." This feeling of guilt, combined with the fear of not being able to accomplish the goal, freezes most of us - freezes us in inactivity. It is a vicious circle as we know in our head that we need to do something, but we hold ourselves back and then the pressure to move ahead creates even more fear and guilt. Yuck! Let's go past that today and leave it all behind. We cannot fix the past, but we can make a different choice. That is what you are doing right now - making a choice. Choose to write the book that lives within you and know that you will write it well and that you will express that creative side of yourself to help make a difference in the world. In other words, "start at start."

You may be full of ideas but do not know how to arrange and organize them so that they become a clear and powerful manuscript. But until you get started, why should you know how to do it? Let's look at it this way, you would not still be reading this if you did not feel, at a deep level, that you have something important to share with the world and you are now ready to take the risk of sharing yourself with that world, so let's get at it.

"The purpose of life is to... matter; to feel it has made some difference that we have lived at all."

Leo Rosten

Chapter 4

OBJECTIVE OR PURPOSE

We are going to consider the words "objective" and "purpose" to be interchangeable for now. The objective of the book, or purpose, is an area that must be addressed at this point. This is one of the most important questions that an author needs to answer before the writing process can begin. There are three categories of purpose - the author's purpose for writing his book, the reader's purpose for reading it and then, there is the purpose of the book itself. We will deal with each of these areas separately.

WRITER'S PURPOSE

Knowing your purpose sets the tone for the entire project and it requires some honesty to reveal all the motivating factors to find the right voice, or is that "write voice?" Why are you moved to write your book? Here are some thoughts, but only you can create a list of reasons that apply to your case. Knowing your own purpose is vital to the integrity and authenticity that will reveal itself to your readers. If you do not know why you are writing your book, the reader will pick up on your lack of direction immediately and put it down. If you are hoping to attract a conventional publisher, agent or media support, your lack of purpose or misdirected aim will put you on the discard pile before they finish the first page.

A writer's purpose can start with just wanting to tell a story based on your own experience, like a recent trip. Perhaps it was something that happened on your way to work that caused you to think twice because it was funny or tragic or unique. Perhaps you have found success in your efforts to achieve your ideal weight, or perhaps the opposite has happened. It might be something more strategic, like wanting to become recognized in your field of endeavor or to be looked at as a spokesperson in your industry, confer expert status or simply give you more credibility. You might have some specialized knowledge about your subject that is important to share with others, a unique perspective about an event that you witnessed or played a role in. You may feel compelled to write a book to change people's minds, inspire action, and explain a concept or point of view. It might be to leave a legacy to your family, friends, and other people who know you.

There are hundreds of reasons to write your book, including the possibility of making money from it. But the key for the aspiring author is to uncover the reasons that apply to them. Finding your writing voice brings a sense of authenticity to your book that readers will connect with or not. Honesty of purpose is reflected on the page and results in increased clarity and makes the process easier and faster from your point of view. If you know <u>why</u> you are doing something, it makes the effort more successful at every level. Keep your purpose posted in front of you as you write. It will bring a sense of mission to your efforts and that results in clarity for the reader and without question makes the author's job easier by keeping the dreaded "writer's block" at bay.

It may seem obvious, but knowing our own purpose along with the reader's and the book's, before you begin writing, results in a much better book. Does it surprise you to learn that many books are written first and then the author attempts to figure out "why" after the fact?

> "If you don't know where you are going, any road will get you there."
>
> Lewis Carroll

READER'S PURPOSE

Let us suppose for a moment that we have created the perfect title, the perfect graphics and cover design, a perfect back cover with fabulous quotes and testimonials, the right price and a marketing campaign that has attracted potential readers just like you imagined. Now let us put ourselves in that potential reader's shoes for a moment. From their point of view, why will they read your book? What is their purpose for purchasing and spending their valuable time reading your musings? This is another area that a successful writer will take into consideration prior to creating a book. It is absolutely key to have enough regard for your readers, to respect the motivations that move them to buy and then to read and, just as importantly, take action based on your writing.

Let's make a few assumptions as we target our writing to a group of people who will become our readers. It is a mistake to think that what we are writing would be informative and valuable to everyone; it is not true - most will have no interest. We might as well accept this upfront and look to the surprisingly small percentage of people who have any interest in our work. It will help us target everything we do to assume that, at best, 5% (and more probably 1%) of the population might be our potential market.

Think about it this way. According to Showbiz Cheatsheet, Stephen King has sold about 700,000 copies of his bestseller, "Carrie," as of 2021. What percentage is that of the American population? Why dilute (or delude) ourselves by attempting to appeal to people who do not know that our book exists, have no interest in the topic, don't read, can't read and, in any case, won't buy? All too often, we try to create something that will appeal to EVERYONE when we should focus and target our work toward that slice of the population who really needs and wants what we offer. We do them a disservice when we try to make our appeal too broad rather than focusing our efforts on our real readers.

As you define your reader's purpose, it will be helpful to define your reader as well. What are the defining characteristics of the ideal reader? You must become very specific here as you create a clear picture of the person who you want to have read your book. Start with demographics to get an idea of age, education, sex, financial status, marital status, health, family, work, geography and all the details that you can create for your mythical reader. Age might be an important element of your decision making. The boomer generation may accept stories, examples, and text-heavy books while generation Y prefers quick, to-the-point information and has little patience for long diatribes. This will help with writing as you craft the correct language, examples, illustrations and the other many details of targeting your book.

There is another area of knowing who you are writing to that is becoming much clearer and more important and that is psychographics. You could consider the 4 dominant personalities of Meyers-Briggs or the DISC system, for instance, and decide which one or two you are writing to. This will determine many things, from writing characteristics to graphic design and layout. Success comes from knowing your audience and what motivates and inspires them, as well as how they prefer to be motivated and inspired. Time spent choosing the right set of parameters for your ideal reader will pay big dividends down the road in both writing and marketing.

So, what are some of the readers' purposes for investing their time and money with you? It could be curiosity, pursuing knowledge, improving themselves, anger, entertainment, fear, joy, the need to change, pure information, or some that may have similar purposes to you as a writer. They too might look to gain insight and credibility in a particular field, or they may have a different point of view than you and are checking out the competition. The better you understand the motivations of your readers, the better you can understand the emotions that motivate them and the better you can write convincingly on your subject. If you know these things, you can create a much better call to action when you get to that stage of the book where you reveal your true mission and how you will accomplish it.

Remember, the reader must receive a benefit from their investment and if you keep in mind that one of their most significant purposes is to attract happiness, you will more fully understand and achieve your role as a writer. You can never lose sight of the fact that the reader buys your book because you have promised them, in your title or subtitle, that this book would make a difference in their lives. Most times, you promise the result would be a positive one for them. Entertainment is a very legitimate purpose for the reader and as a writer, you owe them the opportunity to be entertained as well as informed.

Whether you are blazing new ground or adding new information or ideas to well-traveled territory, your book will be original because it reflects your unique thoughts. You will use your own style of language as a reflection of your personal point of view and your readers will respond in their own unique way. All of this adds up to a distinct voice that offers a unique twist no matter what the topic. There is one more purpose to consider at this time:

BOOK'S PURPOSE

Your purpose as a writer and the book's purpose are not the same thing. The book's purpose is to persuade, cajole, inform, entertain, challenge, create change, motivate a course of action, and show us how to become involved or try something new. Separate yourself from your writer-self and look at the book as a stand-alone entity and create its purpose for being. Pretend that you are a pilot and the book your airplane; your purpose is to guide the plane or book, but the plane or book's purpose is to hold people safely and take them to their destination in comfort. Try to separate the pilot from the plane for a few moments and identify the book's purpose when you are not there to tell the reader what it is about or how it will benefit them by reading it.

Another way to look at this is to imagine your book is a corporation. You probably know that a company is viewed as a separate legal entity; separate from its owners and managers. Think of your book and your relationship to it similarly. Your book is like your company and its purpose for being differs from yours personally.

The book you are writing is a legacy of your thoughts and ideas, but it exists as an entity on its own. Many times, the reader will have no interest in who the author is, but only in the book and its contents. This is especially true of non-fiction writing. Think of how many times you have read a non-fiction book in any field and remembered the author's name, especially if they do not hold any celebrity status. One area of writing that shows the importance of this distinction is in the "How To" area of writing. Showing a person how to reach their ideal weight, change a faucet, or renovate a house, makes the book an entity very distinct from its author.

Chapter 5

UNIQUE PROPOSITION

Writers get blocked or sometimes do not even begin a book because they think that everything that needs to be said on a topic is already out there. This is simply not true. You have a unique proposition, a unique thought process, and a unique perspective on your topic. Your style of writing and the method, order and voice that will be displayed in your book will attract readers who could not relate to previous authors on the same topic.

You can enhance the uniqueness of your writing by reconsidering your reader and determining what you want them to think and what kind of action you want them to take. Your writing is based on a personal experience or passion. Your interest and perspective combine with your qualifications and other personal demographics and psychographic data to offer a viewpoint that differs from any other writer on your topic. You can trust this to produce a book that will always differ from your competitors. Many writers can write multiple books on the same topic because their own knowledge, experiences, point of view and perspective changes to allow them to reach a different audience, or even the same audience, with a new tone and a renewed vigor.

The other thing that happens is information. It is expanding and becoming more accessible at exponential rates, and this gives a writer the opportunity to revisit a topic many times as new ideas, facts, and solutions come to light. You, as an author, will have sources and information available to you that previous writers on the subject were not aware of and, sometimes, they were aware but ignored. In short, we all come to our topics with incredibly unique circumstances and influences that cause us to write our books with language and thoughts completely different from anyone else.

We can now access large amounts of information quickly through the use of different programs lumped together in the category, Artificial Intelligence. In layperson's language, we can significantly reduce the time spent in research. We should realize that we need to corroborate any information we access before accepting it as the truth, regardless of the source. Another book that I have written, "**THE PROSPEROUS PEN: Mastering Freelance Writing for Retirement Riches**," Book 2 of the **EXTRA RETIREMENT INCOME IS SEXY** series, addresses Artificial Intelligence and writing. I quote here,

"So, the question is, can artificial intelligence help you as a freelance writer? The short answer is yes. The longer answer is yes, but you need to learn how to use it to help you. This boils down to creating the right 'prompts' to enter into the search box and then refining until the information you need is useful.

At the time of writing this book, artificial intelligence is creating a firestorm of controversy. Tried, true and established authors, especially those of the fiction variety, seem to take the stance that AI is the devil incarnate. I'm not so sure. New technology has always been challenging on many levels. I recall as a young lad that using an electronic calculator to do math was a mortal sin. I may yet go to hell, especially if my grade 5 teacher, Sister Mary Joseph, knew that I now have one on the phone that I carry in my pocket!

There are some questionable characters out there who are asking an AI app to create stories and then they upload them to various book selling sites and sell them as is. They are creating rubbish and attempting to get rich quick. Here is what I know about using AI as of this time: it has a very useful place to assist in research, outlining and defining concepts, especially difficult to understand things. The key to using it successfully is learning how to ask questions and keep asking them until you get a proper answer. When I was younger, we used to call this part of the world a library and Encyclopedia Britannica. Today, the repository of all information is the internet.

The art of wording inquiries or prompts and then determining how to proceed from there is rapidly becoming a whole new industry and one you might want to learn about. This author recently viewed a question on an AI app that asked it to explain Quantum Physics in language that a 5-year-old would understand. The information it created was amusing, and I learned a lot. Potential clients for your freelance writing services may want you to generate documentation for them faster and more accurately – AI is probably the answer.

Some people, thanks to the media, have decided that it is a new and foreboding technology and insist on showing pictures of scary looking robots from horror movies in their presentations. Here are a few examples of artificial intelligence at work that you may already know: smart home devices like Alexa, Google Home and more, self-driving cars, Netflix and Spotify recommendations, auto complete in Google Search and messaging apps, Facebook and Instagram, Spell and Grammar check in Word. We have been using it for years.

A recommendation: if you decide to use apps like Chat/GPT and any of the many others, it is essential that you take into consideration any ethical and moral issues. Amazon is now requiring writers to acknowledge if AI was used and how it was used to create books. This author thinks we will come to accept the value and input of AI soon and look at it as a useful tool to increase productivity.

The internet and social media are swirling with articles on artificial intelligence including "how-to's" and warnings. Therefore, if you are thinking about accessing its help, it would be a good idea to keep up with current thought."

Your book will appeal to both a different audience and differently than those written previously, and that audience will connect with your writing and hear your unique voice in a new way. This is a good time to take a break and think about what the central message of your book is. You could follow this by writing out a paragraph or two that defines your message, your purpose, your reason for being as it relates to your book and its topic.

Chapter 6

QUALIFICATIONS

The qualifications to write on a particular topic can come to us from our academic pursuits to hands-on experience and everything in between. Depending on the topic and those same qualifications, you, as a writer, will show your knowledge and authenticity in many ways. You would not write a travel story about an exotic locale without having visited it because there would be no ring of authenticity and your reader would spot the inconsistency quickly. Just the same, you do not require specific training to write your travel story. Write it from the heart and check your facts to make sure that your reader is not led astray. You can also be open to using your personal experiences to create a work of fiction such as a short story, magazine article or full-blown novel. Allowing your personal interests to mix with facts and a unique perspective gives you the perfect mix to create something enjoyable and perhaps saleable.

There will be certain topics that cry out for specific credentials but that does not prevent you from writing a personal perspective book. For instance, depending on your aim, you might require a medical degree to write about health issues, unless you have a personal connection to a specific problem. Perhaps a family member, friend or you yourself, have a hands-on story about an issue, like weight loss, and you can write from that hands-on situation - that is your qualification. In something like this, you will want to be careful about how you include unsubstantiated opinions and be clear on the difference between facts and opinions. In today's world, facts are easily checked, and someone will, especially if your book becomes successful, so keep that in mind.

This does not prevent you from taking a position that is unconventional or controversial, but from a writing point of view, separate facts from conjecture and be sure that the reader is aware of which one is which. This kind of book has legitimacy with the reading public and can be a tremendous force for change. You do not need to be illiterate to write about illiteracy and the issues associated with it. Just make sure that any statistics that you present are double-checked and up to date and then allow your personal passion for the topic to come through to the reader. Passion for the topic may be your strongest qualification and that makes it the perfect reason to write on the topic.

Chapter 7

KEYWORDS

In your search for information, either online or elsewhere, it would be a good idea to keep a list of those words that keep coming up repeatedly. This list will help you tremendously as you consider a title for your book. The other place where these search words become valuable is in the world of search engine optimization. Having appropriate and powerful keywords in your title and book description will help potential readers find your writing. There are some writing factories that overuse this method and overload their work with specific keywords, but fortunately, Google and the other search engines constantly alter their algorithms to counter this blatant attempt to influence searchers. Stay true to your topic, but be aware of the use and power of keywords to help your results.

Having a working title near the beginning of your project helps you, as the writer, to stay focused and so this will be a good time to introduce you to the seven characteristics of an excellent title.

1. Juxtaposition - this is more important if your book is going to be found on a traditional bookstore shelf. The books that stand out have titles that do not seem to fit on the shelf the buyer is looking at. The potential buyer walks into a store looking for something on Italian cooking and on the shelf with the other cookbooks, they cannot help but notice one with a title that just does not seem to fit. "**You put WHAT in the Sauce?**" or, "**My Pasta is Criminal**," are probably more attention getting than "**Cooking Italian**." The point is to get noticed enough to have the potential reader pick up your book instead of the one next to it.

2. Address the issue, problem or need that you are writing about. Give the reader the opportunity to know what you are writing about - nothing cutesy - but at least one word in the title should mention your topic. This might be in the subtitle rather than the main one.

3. Keywords - once again we talk about search engine optimization but if you can get a few search-able words connected to your major topic, it will help to get found in the various search engines and databases. There is much more to this science than we are going to cover here, and it takes much more than just a word or two in the title, but that will at least support your further efforts to create and locate your audience. Do not get carried away in this need for SEO, but simply be aware, especially if you intend to self-publish. You will find lots of help in an app called **Publisher Rocket**.

4. Promise - your title should inform potential readers of something they will stop doing, start doing or start doing differently because of reading your book. Therefore, your audience may buy your book because they want something as a payoff for their hard-earned dollars. They will pay for your book in exchange for receiving a benefit for themselves. There are personal benefits to reading an altruistic book that offers world change because it makes the reader feel better.

5. Tease the reader with something provocative, eye catching, controversial, shocking, humorous,

unexpected, challenging or over the top in the title. You are seeking attention in the face of thousands of other titles that are competing with you. Therefore, I created the title, **_EXTRA RETIREMENT INCOME IS SEXY_**, for a recently published series. Some authors have had outstanding success with NURDS. This is the art of creating a word that does not exist but mashes other words into a new one - sometimes it will even enter the language if the book is very successful. e.g., **Freakonomics** or a word that is totally unfamiliar like, **Outliers**.

6. Alliteration or rhyme will help the title roll off the reader's tongue; helps make it repeatable and memorable. Be careful here because, depending on your topic, a cutesy title could easily work against you. You will want to test this idea with an objective advisor or two before you commit to it.

7. No superfluous words. Keep the title as tight as you can, try using a verb or action word in the title - some recent releases use just one verb as the main title and rely on the subtitle or the author's name to carry the day. This is not a hard and fast rule since there are many exceptions that have long

titles, but the first couple of words are the key to remembering the book.

Bonus: try to work numbers into the title if you can such as, the 5 habits, the 7 secrets, the 3 most important... You get the idea; it is part of the promise that you, as the author, are making to the reader and you are telling them what to expect because of reading your book. This has worked very well for some multi-million selling books and it might for yours, too.

The bottom line is that you cannot work all these characteristics into your title, but the more you can use, the better chance you will have of being noticed. The idea is to encourage your potential reader to take your book off the shelf, examine the cover, and decide to investigate further. And just one last caution; if you are going to sell your book to a traditional publisher, they will have the last word on any title. Spend some time in your local bookstore perusing the titles both in your genre and outside and see if some ideas occur to you.

Chapter 8

BLITZ

Most writers accumulate all sorts of "stuff" that includes sources of information, random newspaper articles, books, maps, pictures, videos, charts, reports and a myriad of other important research that we try to keep in a safe place in case we write that book. Today, we often fill file folders on our computers with online research like blogs and subscriptions and reports, all in the hope of finding it again when we are ready to write. We have dozens of sources to quote, research documentation to substantiate our thoughts and links to websites around the world that we have been saving for this day.

We have all experienced the "cleaning blitz" usually performed just before listing our houses for sale. What is the thing that everyone who has ever done this says? "We should have done this long ago! Let's never let it get this bad again."

We are going to embark on an information blitz and spend a day getting our information houses in order. Dedicate a full day to locating all the relevant information, deciding whether to keep it for this project, assign it to some future project or dump it in the trash bin. Be brutal and stay on target. What are you writing about? Will this be important to this project? If not, do something about it! I would guess that you will have a combination of online documents and hard copy sources and somehow, we need to pull this together so we can find it when needed. One way to start is with a physical file box and start loading all the material that we need into it. This could be other books (with passages marked), videos, pictures, random notebooks, newspaper clippings, journals and cocktail napkins - anything that applies to the writing project. Keep it in one place for the time being.

Next is the computer documentation. I suggest you create a new file folder loosely named after the working title of your book and copy anything that is relevant to the new folder. Organization is not as important as accumulation. Later, we will get to the actual organization and know what to do with all this information. The point now is to create a repository for all the research and important materials that will be necessary to create your book. Sometimes, an empty space on the living room floor may serve as an assembly point for your items. A lot of time is wasted looking for just the right source of information when we should be writing. This will give us the confidence to know where to look when the time comes.

Create a "blitz day" so that you can get an idea of what you already have and an idea of what you might still need. If there are a few more sources or items that will absolutely be required, then now is the time to get them. Perhaps you will need the cooperation and material of other people. Now is the time to ask for anything that will take some time to assemble or receive permission to quote.

Chapter 9

ORGANIZE

I smile to myself as I write this: telling an author to get organized is almost as bad as telling a writer to be more creative. No matter what the topic, no matter how dry or academic, we need to tap into the creative part of ourselves to write something that others want to read. This requires an artist's touch and, most times, organization tears the heart out of artistry. However, there is just no way around the procedure that needs to take place now and that is to get organized to get creative!

Take a recipe card or an index card and write, in 10 words or fewer, the answer to this question, **"What's your book about?"** Don't explain why you are writing it and all the other details about how, or what, or when or who. Just answer as clearly as possible, **"What's your book about?"** Do this exercise now before you go on. Please don't decide to read to the end of the book and then come back to this exercise. DO IT NOW!

Did you find this difficult to do in 10 words or fewer? Most people find they want to explain everything and here is another saying, "Explanations kill deals." We live in a world of 15 second commercials and this is your chance for a 15 second book pitch. If you insist on making it longer than that, your audience will drift off. We will come back to this point later, but I want you to get a feel for creating a short answer to a question that you will be asked for the rest of your life. You might just as well make it interesting and succinct. After all, you could be talking to someone who has an in-law who is a publisher - you never know.

FIELD TRIP

Now, you have a working idea of the topic of your book and maybe even an answer to what it is about. It is time for a field trip - literally. Creating a book is truly a right-brained activity and you need to stimulate that side of your brain to create the book that readers want to read. This is a good time to call a halt to the left-brained organizational freak that lives in some of us - make a physical break. Somewhere near where you live there is a park and walking or hiking trails. Please do not substitute a walk through the city streets; we really need to connect with trees, grass and animal life like birds and insects and others. Study after study shows that when we link ourselves with nature, our creativity spikes, and we naturally see more clearly what lies ahead. This is an exercise that needs to be done alone, so lace up those running shoes, put on some appropriate walking wear and grab a half dozen more index cards and a pen.

After you have walked for a while and warmed up your creative brain with some deep breaths and used your ears to hear the sounds of nature, your nose to smell the air, grass and water and your eyes to see the beauty that surrounds you: knowing what your book is about, break it down into sections - I strongly suggest 10. Stop and write a word or two to describe the topic of each section until you reach ten. Here's the deal: the walk is not over until you have created at least 10 topics that you will have to cover in order to do your book and its readers justice. The number ten may seem arbitrary, but it allows you to show your breadth of knowledge on your topic and forces you to give wide consideration to what you need to write about.

There is a possibility that you have just created 10 chapters of your book and the table of contents. We are not sure at this point, but when you have completed this field trip, you should have a pretty good understanding of what your book needs to include to cover your subject with some authority. It is important to establish the fact that you have a broad understanding of your subject and if you can break it into ten subtopics, that will show and establish your expertise. There is magic in the number 10, and we will explain it shortly. Back home now and time to get to work on that enormous pile of information that is residing on the living room floor.

Using your 10 subtopics as a guide, split your information into that number of piles on the floor. There may be some hard choices to make as you decide when and where some of the information belongs. You may change your mind later, but for now, use a broad-stroke approach to putting research in its most logical place. When you have finished that process, move onto the computerized information by creating 10 sub-folders and moving information, URL's, blogs, bookmarks, etc. to one or more subs as it pertains to the topic. Yes, there may be some duplication, but you will become more disciplined with where and how you divide your information as you proceed. Resist the need to create and conduct more research to add to your storehouse. It may not seem like it, but you already have enough to get started on the writing. You will do additional research, if it is necessary, when you reach that stage of the writing project - NOT NOW.

You have just accomplished a big job that will pay huge dividends later, so treat yourself to a glass of wine and a movie - you are rapidly becoming an author.

Chapter 10

OUTLINE

You have created 10 topics and have assembled all your existing information, sources and ideas into separate folders, boxes and piles, so it is now time to think about the order of your topics. Look at your index cards on which you wrote your original 10 topics and transfer each one to its own page of printer paper. You can make it all organized and neat by using your computer to make a nice bold headline on each page or just use a permanent marker - whatever works for you. Create a separate page for each item and DO NOT NUMBER the pages. I now use what is called "painter's masking tape" and put each of the 10 pages up on the wall in my office and rearrange until I get them into a logical sequence for my book. You might edit the topic headings, adding or subtracting a word. You might also realize that there are some new ideas percolating about each of your topics, and the best way to approach this is to jot down the new ideas on each page under the headings. This is the next part of the process after reordering your topics into a logical progression that will make more sense in your book.

For each topic page, think a little deeper about what you will need to include and add three or four sub-topics on each page. These are called "must-haves" and refer to the fact that for each of your major sub-topics, you will need to delve a little deeper and reveal the 3 - 4 things that you must cover in each area to complete your thoughts on this section. You should now have what is called a map board for all 10 major topics that includes the general heading for the area, followed by 3 - 4 sub-areas that must be included in order to give the section real depth of knowledge and explanation. Some people graduate to a large piece of poster board paper and include other documents, pictures and so forth to create a highly visual game plan for each section they will write about.

So, here is what we have to date; an organized map board or guideline for each major section of your book, which includes the major points to be covered in each section. You have now created a broad enough view of your topic (10 topics) and established some in-depth coverage (3 - 4 must-haves) to write a book that will be convincing, revealing and informative. Finding an order of information that you are pleased with may not happen for a while - do not worry about that. Number your major topics/map boards (1 through 10) with a pencil so that it is easy to rearrange as you move forward. Tape these map boards onto the wall in your office or writing space so that you have a visual layout of your book project. It really helps to keep things organized when you can see the entire plan at once. Doing it this way also helps when rearranging the information itself, as certain segments make more sense elsewhere in your book.

What about that "magic of 10" phrase that was used a few pages ago? Let's do the math - 10 major topics and 3 - 4 must-haves for each topic means that you have 40 chunks of information that need to be written for your book. This might equate to chapters and sub-headings; we just do not know at this stage, and it is not too important right now. You have created 40 writing targets that are now available to you to organize your research around and set as individual pieces of writing to be created and then blended into your book. Depending upon several logistical factors, including time and volume of material, you could see yourself setting each of these targets as a goal for each day of writing and just maybe, you would have the bulk of your book written in about 40 days! No, this is not impossible, especially once you review the rest of the material that we will share.

Consider reorganizing your 10 piles and folders of information to assign them to your 40 mini topics, although there is usually a fair amount of over-lap depending on what you are writing about. It is worth realizing that much of this now becomes a bit of a moving target as you amass written notes and short point form post-its and other important things to remember as the actual writing draws ever closer. This is a time of great liquidity as thoughts occur to you about what must be included, and you change your mind about where to include it.

This is a natural process that unfolds organically, so allow it to happen if it does. You will have many outside sources of information by this time, and it is now important to create a detailed list to credit other authors, reports, articles, videos, and so on. As you come across important items, create a "source" folder to track complete information including page numbers, publishers, ISBNs, and anything else to give your quote authority and credence and also, so that you can find the relevant material yourself when the time comes.

There is another reason for creating a map or information board for each section. When you are several weeks into your writing process, it is easy to forget whether you have covered a topic, and that piece of information might fit in to several areas. With a game plan in front of you, it is easy to see immediately if you have previously included the information and where. It sure beats rereading everything to find a single paragraph or fact.

This is a good time to introduce a quick outlining technique to get you started down the right path with your non-fiction book. For each of your 40 topics, consider setting up a small outline that provides these four items.

- a note about the information in this section

- a statement that defines your thought, idea, or opinion

- a fact or two or three to support your statement

- an example that illustrates your point

This very rudimentary outline will help you see the details in the bigger picture and it is easy to adapt to specific projects, but if you are trying to convince readers to take some sort of action, this will help you make your case.

Chapter 11

KNOWLEDGE

Time for another field trip, but one that will take a bit more planning and one that is very important to the success of your writing efforts. I should add that this field trip is one of the fun parts of this program and clients have had amazing things happen during it. I recommend you do this field trip several times to get the maximum benefit. First, a little preparation that will make the process even more valuable to what is coming up - mainly the writing of your book.

Once again, answer the question, **"What's your book about?"**

Here are a few tips for answering this question:

- 10 words or fewer

- identify your topic

- identify a problem or challenge

- identify a solution that you propose

- remember to express a benefit to the listener/reader

This sounds like a tall order to cram into 10 words or fewer, but now is a perfect time to begin looking for examples of this in action. Where would you find authors describing what their books are about? Yes, that's right, on the dustcover of their books, in newspaper or magazine reviews, on their websites and blogs. Check your bookcase or your e-reader and begin reading (this is research) the descriptions of a dozen non-fiction books. The author always writes these, and they may be how he or she answers the question, **"What's your book about?"** You might just as well learn from someone who has already done it, especially when it is free. One thing you will learn right away is that some do it well (you can tell because you feel like buying or reading their book) and some do a remarkably poor job of it.

This may be an ongoing job as an author, to create the perfect, short, and dynamic description of their book. It will guide much more than prospective readers, reviewers, and publishers. It will have an incredible impact on your writing procedure when you have a very clear description of what you are writing about. This may be the most important thing you do to ensure the success of your project. I urge you to continue working at this until it is the best you can do and then we can move on to the field trip. Trying out your answer with people you know may or may not be a good idea. You are the judge. Trying it out on people at work or at social engagements may bring some new insight, but the best feedback will come from total strangers, since most of your prospective readers will be strangers. You are trying to gauge whether people can relate to your topic and are interested in your solution. If you get their attention and they relate, they might buy your book. If they do not connect, then there is no way they will buy unless they are forced to because of being your brother-in-law.

Alright, the perfect 10 words or less description of what your book is about is freshly memorized and burning a hole in your sharing gene - let's go out and test it. You will find a brick and mortar bookstore - one where you are unknown - and you are going to engage one of the best research assistants you will never hire. Take a small notebook with you and be prepared to learn a lot. First, be able to describe your own book, using much the same language that you just created, and go looking for that same book. It will work very well when a store employee sees you walk into the store looking bewildered and needing help. They have a need and mission to provide help, so they will ask, "Can I help you find something?"

This next part is very important as you crank up your powers of observation and tell this helpful employee that you are looking for a book, and then describe the one you are going to write. Naturally, you will not share the part about you writing a book but describe in as short a way as possible what your book is about. You might have to be a little imaginative here if you are describing a weight-loss book and only weigh 90 pounds yourself. Make up a bit of story if necessary. One of my clients usually goes in and uses an opening that she is a life coach and is looking for something for a specific client and describes the issues she wants to write about. She tells the clerk that she would like to buy a book for this fictitious client to help them. Several things are going to happen quickly, and you must carefully observe your "research assistant's" eyes. If they understand what kind of book you are seeking, they will express it quickly with wide open eyes and a smile and almost grab you by the arm and march you to the shelf and book in question.

If only that would happen every time, then we would all be absolute writing geniuses or, more importantly, marketing geniuses. It is possible that you will not receive this kind of reception the first few times you try it. Instead, you might get a look of bewilderment from the store employee and a question like, "Do you have a title or author's name?" Here is what this look of confusion and similar question really means - you have not explained what you are writing about. The answer to the question, "**What's your book about?**" is not clear enough. The clerk should be able to understand immediately the store section your book can be found in and what subsection. She may not have a title at her fingertips but should understand clearly what your book search is about and be able to lead you to the shelf where you will find it. Here's the kicker: if you cannot tell someone else what you are writing about, then you do not know yourself.

Following this section, I am going to give you some more ideas of places to do similar research, but for now, it is advisable to not start your request by telling the store clerk what section it will be found in. Let them decide based on your description efforts. You might be surprised when they suggest a section that you didn't know existed or a place in the store where you would attract much more exposure and not be just another book in a long list of the same. Knowing what genre your book belongs in is a gigantic step in your success as an author and it may not be what you originally thought. It is also possible that you might want it to be in a specific section, but what you are describing belongs elsewhere. This is incredibly valuable intelligence. One other point, if the helpful sales associate/research assistant nods off during your description - see the section on 10 words or fewer - really!

Alright, let's assume that at some point you have described your book well enough for the associate to take you to a section of the store. Pay very close attention to where he takes you, the language he uses and the exact location within the section. This will tell you what exactly you have described to this person. Is it what you thought it was? No need to argue with the salesperson, since they have only done what you asked. If you are not where you want to be, then thank them and go back to work. Work on your topic and what you want to write about. If it is not clear to an experienced bookstore employee, how do you suppose they will ever be able to help future customers find your book? One other thing; the store will not create a separate section for your book - unfortunately, you need to conform to the existing categories.

More importantly, realize that you have not defined your topic well enough for you to write about it. Eventually, you will have your book description completed so that a bookstore associate can take you to the right section (it could be a different section than you originally planned) and have your search narrowed down to the right shelf in the section. Thank your research assistant and allow them to leave and serve other customers, and you can proceed with the rest of your work. You have just been introduced to the competitive books on your topic and this is a good thing. If there are no books dealing with your topic, then perhaps there is no market for your book. This is important to consider. Are there any prospective readers for your book? It is also important to consider currently if your readership is fairly narrow and not accessible through conventional bookstores, but through online marketing or some other means instead.

There is more to learn in the bookstore by looking at other books in your section, like titles, covers, colors and interior book layouts. What appeals to you? Look at various font styles, the use of white space, illustrations, and charts. Most of the books will have only the spine facing toward the buyer. What makes you pick one off the shelf and not another? These are all important to know about as you move forward with your own project. This is an exercise that should be repeated a few times to confirm your topic and its findability. Review this section before conducting your field trip and get as much information from the exercise as possible. Write down your findings, take pictures of book covers, shelves, anything that will be important in the future. You must rework your book description until it actually works, and you get the results you want. Adjust your target until you and your potential audience know what you are writing about.

Going to a large bookstore will cause an incredible amount of information to guide your writing journey. You could also include the main library in your town and glean a similar amount of knowledge. Another fabulous source of information can be found online through Amazon. Use their search box to inquire about books with similar subjects as yours and keep targeting more search words. To dig deeper into categories and keywords, investigate a program called **Publisher Rocket**. You can find more information about that program and several other essential writing tools on my website (RobertJBannon.com) on the page, Tools for Writers.

Unfortunately, many would-be authors wait until their book is finished to conduct an exercise like this – it's too late then, unless you are going to rewrite the book based on your findings – why waste that much time? Do it first – go on your field trip early and find the answer to one of your most important questions, "**What's Your Book About?**"

Chapter 12

BLUEPRINT

Following your successful field trip, it is time to take another look at your topics and subtopics and make any adjustments based on your fact-finding mission. Sometimes it will be necessary to rearrange the order, remove or replace subtopics, and so on. You might find it necessary to recreate some of your map boards. This organizational process will create your writing blueprint and create clarity in your mind, thus assisting your reader to find clarity in your message. Here is a quick tip in case you get stuck in trying to create your subtopics: look at the principal topic and make sure you are answering the following questions: who, what, where, when, why and how. The old journalist's guide to a good story outline will work for your book and help reveal what your reader needs to know to be clear on what you are presenting.

I recently published a series of books for seniors and retirees who want to add some extra income to their lives. One suggestion is writing books, and it includes some information that will be relevant here.

"Let's look a little deeper at some ideas to see how you can become a successful author.

EBOOKS AND GUIDES

The first step is creating a product.

Creating and selling non-fiction ebooks and guides can be a rewarding venture. Here are key elements to consider for success:

Choose a Target Audience:

Identify a specific audience for your ebook. Knowing your target audience will help you tailor the content to meet their needs and preferences.

Select a Niche or Topic:

Choose a niche or topic that aligns with your expertise or interests. It should be something that your target audience is interested in learning more about.

Interesting Title and Cover Design:

Create a captivating title and an eye-catching cover design. These elements play a crucial role in attracting potential readers. There are many sources online for creating covers, including Fiverr and many DIY software options like **BookBrush**.

Quality Content:

Provide valuable and well-researched content. Ensure that your writing is clear, concise, and engaging. Readers should find practical solutions or gain insights from your ebook.

Professional Formatting:

Pay attention to formatting. Ensure that someone professionally formatted your ebook for readability on various devices. Consider hiring a designer if needed.

Atticus is a high-quality formatting app you can buy to do it yourself.

Amazon's Kindle software will help with this, as will Draft2Digital, or look at Sqribble for an easy-to-use method of ebook creation.

Use Visuals and Graphics:

Incorporate relevant visuals, charts, and graphics to enhance the reader's understanding. Visual elements can break up text and make the content more engaging.

Interactive Elements:

Depending on the topic, consider adding interactive elements, such as quizzes, checklists, or links to additional resources. This can enhance reader engagement.

Proofreading and Editing:

Edit and proofread your ebook thoroughly to eliminate grammatical errors and ensure a polished final product. Consider hiring a professional editor if possible or investigate buying an app like **ProWritingAid**.

Choose the Right Format:

Decide on the format of your e-book. Common formats include PDF, EPUB, and MOBI. Note that Kindle is no longer supporting MOBI. Consider offering your ebook in multiple formats, digital, print and audio to cater to different reading preferences.

Effective Marketing Copy:

Craft interesting marketing copy for your ebook. Use persuasive language to highlight the benefits readers will gain by purchasing and reading your content.

Pricing Strategy:

Determine the pricing strategy for your ebook. Research similar ebooks in your niche to understand market standards. You may choose to offer promotional pricing initially.

Distribution Platforms:

Select the platforms where you'll sell your e-book. Popular options include Amazon's, Kindle Direct Publishing (KDP), Smashwords, IngramSpark, Direct2Digital, Sqribble, and Gumroad.

Build an Author Platform:

Establish an online presence as an author. Create a website or author page where readers can learn more about you and your other works.

Effective Promotion:

Develop a marketing plan to promote your ebook. This could include social media promotion, email marketing, collaborations with influencers, or guest blogging.

Collect and Use Reviews:

Encourage readers to leave reviews. Positive reviews can significantly impact sales. Consider offering early copies to influencers for reviews.

Continuous Updates.

If applicable, plan for updates to keep your content relevant. This can encourage previous readers to recommend the updated version to others.

Remember, successful non-fiction ebook creation and sales often involve an ongoing process of improvement. Stay connected with your audience, gather feedback, and use it to enhance your future works."

Excerpted from **DESIGNING WEALTH: A Retiree's Guide to More Income and Creative Fulfillment** - Book 5 in the **EXTRA RETIREMENT INCOME IS SEXY** series.

by Robert J Bannon

Chapter 13

TRIGGER SENTENCES

"It was a dark and stormy night...?" Do you remember that old cliché sentence? Does it encourage you to read on? On television shows and movies, the opening scene compels you to continue viewing by creating mystery, humor, controversy, a wild and crazy action scene (think James Bond). Sometimes the opening simply encourages the viewer to continue watching by promising to reveal something soon. In the book world, we call this a "trigger sentence." A trigger sentence is one that will "trigger" the reader to continue on and find out more. Another excellent exercise is to watch for trigger sentences in the opening line of emails, books, movies, newspaper features, everywhere. You will need to create a trigger sentence for each of your topics, chapters, or sections.

"Trigger sentences" have some characteristics that are important to incorporate:

- a trigger sentence reveals some information ahead

- a trigger sentence is punchy

- a trigger sentence is controversial

- a trigger sentence has impact

- a trigger sentence defines the topic

- a trigger sentence is powerful

- a trigger sentence is compelling

- a trigger sentence makes a promise to the reader

- a trigger sentence teases

- a trigger sentence defines the coming chapter or section

To find great trigger sentences, look at the work of Seth Godin or Tim Ferriss, both best-selling authors and consummate marketers. Here are a few examples from Timothy Ferriss, "***The 4 - Hour Workweek***" selected from random sections:

"To do or not to do."

"Fear comes in many forms, and we usually don't call it by its four letter name."

"If you're an employee, spending time on nonsense is, to some extent, not your fault."

"Blaming idiots for interruptions is like blaming clowns for scaring children - they can't help it."

"The key to having more time is doing less, and there are two paths to getting there..."

and from Seth Godin, "***All Marketers are Liars***"

"I'm angry when babies are killed by deceitful marketers."

"People buy books (millions of them every year) without knowing what's inside."

"A bullfrog's brain weighs about twenty-four grams."

"The news on television isn't "true." It can't be."

The first sentence in Godin's book, "I have no intention of telling you the truth."

As you can see, you can take other commonly known sayings, quotes, advertising messages - anything - and rewrite it to fit your book and message.

The familiarity of other quotes will actually help your reader to identify with your message. The point is to create curiosity, anger, fear - something that will cause the reader to keep reading. Well-written works of fiction can serve as another source of good "trigger sentences." Consider looking there and adjusting as necessary to create your own triggers and compel your readers to keep going. Once you start down this trail, you will find potential trigger sentences everywhere, and that is another good reason for carrying a small notebook. You can always create a text, email or otherwise record your ideas on the go, on your cell phone. Some people can go through each of their topics and write the first sentence before they begin the actual detailed writing process, so whatever works for you and however you are inspired, trigger sentences are another key ingredient to your success.

"I didn't mean to throw him off the roof after reading his book. OK, maybe I did." RJB :)

You should now have an excellent working blueprint of how the information in your book will be laid out. Your blueprint should remain active and organic in the sense that you can freely add or move sections, make a note to research or find more material and a thousand other things that will improve your writing process. There is, besides these practical matters, a sense of calm and professionalism that descends in knowing that you have a complete picture of what you want to accomplish. It really is an organized, self-coaching program that allows you to move forward with confidence.

Chapter 14

OBSERVE

If you have accomplished the tasks outlined previously (and this is not just your first read-through) you can and should begin the writing process. Some quick advice before you begin:

- do not write the introduction or forward until you have completed the book

- start with the easiest section to write

- handwriting or computer, always double line spacing

- make time for reading quality writing - in another genre

At the beginning of this book, I quoted some famous people, and this is very popular with writers of fiction and non-fiction alike. You can buy books of quotations, search them online and simply keep a record of quotes that inspire you. It is obvious but must be stated, if you are going to quote someone, you must credit them. You rarely require permission to use a quote if you reveal the source. There is another option, and that is to create your own quotable quotes. It is not as hard as it sounds, nor do you need to be "famous" to be quoted. It is a very enjoyable exercise to sit down with some empty index cards in a coffee shop or while waiting for a lunch partner, pick a topic and then write a few quotes of your own. Keep them short, with a point. They can be a play on words, even someone else's words, or a popular or recognizable saying, advertising slogan - you can find your inspiration everywhere. Now that you are conscious of this possibility, you really will find inspiration everywhere. Keep an eye open and become an observer of words, phrases, sayings, and song lyrics.

Conscious awareness leads to congruence - that is bordering on a quotable phrase - but here is what I mean: if you are buying a new car and have decided on a make and model (this is the conscious awareness part) something happens as you drive around town. We have all experienced this phenomenon as we realize how many similar makes and models are on the road with us. We probably did not even notice them prior to our decision to buy the vehicle, but now they seem to be everywhere (this is the congruence part). I also like to refer to this phenomenon as the yellow car syndrome. The same thing happens with creating a series of quotes, especially if we want to create a few on a particular topic; we will find either similar quotes or ones that we can adapt to our own words. Try it and pick a specific topic to create quotes for and then keep your eyes open. If you are unsure of its originality, enter your newfound quote into the Google search box and, if it has already been used, you will confirm it. This is a terrific example of the Law of Attraction in action.

When you went on your recent field trip, what other information did you accumulate through observation? Are you now clear on exactly where to find your book? What mainstream genre will you be in? On what shelf in a bookstore will your book be placed? Why will a potential reader/buyer choose your book? What is the competition? How many books deal with your specific topic? What are their core messages? Are they recent publications, old or a combination? In your observation process, it is vital that you repeat this procedure for online offerings as well. Where will your book be placed on the Amazon, Barnes and Noble, Kobo, i-Tunes, etc. site, what genre, what about competitive books and so on? Using the app, Publisher Rocket mentioned earlier will help you with this process. If this is your first read-through of this book, mark this page and come back to it more than once - it is paramount to your future book selling success.

Besides understanding this "observation process" for your own writing needs, you will need this information available to you if you decide to attract an agent or publisher. They will expect that you have done your research before approaching them. If you cannot show your understanding of your market niche, then you can expect their rejection letter when they get around to it. Don't give them an opportunity to throw your hard work on to the "no thanks" pile by not doing your part of the job. And yes, this, like marketing, is the author's responsibility. Taking on this assignment will cause you to write a better book and a more targeted publication

- the agents and publishers already know this. If there are any gaps in your observations, repeat your field trips from the beginning including the answer to the question, "What's your book about?" Be able to create a plausible request to the bookstore employee that will allow them to take you to the shelf where you will find your book in the future. Create the correct search words for the various companies like Amazon that result in you being guided to books that address your topic.

Alright, what are you waiting for? Let's start doing some writing!

- I looked for the quote, "*Conscious awareness leads to congruence,*" and I can't find it anywhere online so, I guess it's mine. If you want to use it, go ahead. Just don't forget to credit it.[1]

1.

Chapter 15

OUTPUT

Let's make those forty topics that you created earlier work their magic for us. You should have a map board for each of your topics, or more accurately, sub-topics and now is the time to tape one on the wall in front of your writing area - this is your first target. Review the information and thoughts that you created about this item and begin the writing process. A short word here about the actual procedure is important. Begin each topic with a trigger sentence. If you have not already created one for the section, then now is the time to do it. Remember, this sentence is a hook, in marketing terms, and creates a need in the reader to go further, to learn about your thoughts, to want more information. Review the material in this book on trigger sentences and be constantly vigilant about improving yours.

I recommend strongly that you create a one-hour time block in your day that is sacrosanct in the sense that you will not allow yourself to be disturbed. Turn off the social networking sites, email, and phone; close the office door, whatever it takes to dedicate one hour to writing your book. The difference between those people who say they want to write a book and those few that do is this one hour of space or time that they protect like a mother bear protecting her cubs. Other than obvious corrections for spelling or missed caps etc., please do not spend this valuable time in any kind of editing process. This is creative time set aside for writing, not editing or research. Refer to your map board for this topic and use the time for producing the book that you know is inside you.

You need tremendous discipline to finish a book. The fanciful stories about waking in the middle of the night and feeling the creative force leak out through your fingertips to the keyboard in some sort of movie-induced dream sequence are fairy tales. There is no substitute for the focused time spent following the plans that you have created and working forward, one sentence, one hour, one section at a time. Notwithstanding this, there will be times when you wake up with the perfect phrase and more and will need to record them immediately before they slip into the recesses of your mind - get up or write it in the notebook beside your bed.

Knowing your ideal reader is now more important than ever. Have you considered their personality type:

- Do they prefer a text heavy format, or are they more likely to prefer bullet points and charts?

- Will your book pages include artwork and lots of white space, with bold titles and other things that appeal to a reader who has little time and is more focused on getting to the results than reading the verbiage?

- Is your ideal reader a person who is more comfortable reading the entire story (in a non-fiction sense) and knowing all the background and details?

How you create your book depends totally on who your potential reader is. Most writers write to themselves and so are content to create a format that is self-appealing rather than thinking about the combination of their information and their ideal reader and using an approach that appeals to them.

Some books will attempt to combine different formats to appeal to a broad range of different reading styles, all between the same covers. It may be possible and preferable to create a second book using the same basic information, but presenting it differently to a fresh set of readers. In today's changing book environment, consideration might be given to offering different formatting and writing techniques if your content crosses personality, generational and delivery (e-readers vs. hard copy) vehicles. "Know your reader" is more important now than ever and knowing the delivery style that appeals to them must now be taken into consideration. For example, this book would lend itself to at least three distinct personality types and delivery vehicles. Can you name them and can you see the possibilities for your own book?

Another thought while we are in the writing process; if the opening sentence is vital to persuading your reader to continue turning the pages, then the last sentences of a section are vital to setting that stage. In a non-fiction book and especially one that attempts to instruct, it is advisable to restate the premise of the section just completed and then to establish a reason for the reader to move to the next section. Once again, in marketing terms, a teaser to help promote the next idea that is presented and encourages your reader to keep going. You can often look to good fiction writing for examples of how an author sets the stage for the next chapter. These are ideas you can incorporate to make your book more readable.

You have approximately forty subtopics to cover and if you wrote one topic per day, the bulk of your book would be complete in about six weeks. Alright, I have not allowed for any downtime, any longer writing chunks, sick days, vacations, Christmas, the birth of a child, unexpected company or the coming of the apocalypse, but then again, neither do most serious writers. It may surprise you to learn just how disciplined many full-time writers are and how they guard their writing time and space against outside intrusions. You might also be right to inform me you are not a full-time writer, but my suggestion is one hour per day, without exception. To be a writer, you must write. The more you write, the more you can write and the more you can write, the faster and better you get at it.

The target market for this book is the non-writer and the person who wants to write a book but has never done so before, is without a master's degree in literature and maybe skipped a few English classes in high school. I know that person very well and it is to them I address this paragraph. Make the daily commitment to write for an hour, and I promise you will be amazed at how quickly your book comes together. I have asked you to ignore the niceties of grammatical construction, punctuation, even spelling and other technical writing procedures for the sake of getting your thoughts, ideas and information on to the page. We will deal with how to handle those things in the next section. For now, write every day, including weekends and vacations. Create a time and space that belongs to the dream that you have given in to, the dream of being an author.

Chapter 16

KNOW-HOW

Does an author need to know everything necessary about the book creation process before she creates her own book? Absolutely not! To think that you must have complete knowledge about all the ins and outs of this business is a total waste of time. The information is available when needed and, if necessary, you can hire people to help you through most of the processes involved. The most important part of creating your book is the courage to put your own ideas and thoughts down on paper. Your creativity, unique perspective and voice are the essential ingredients to creating a book. Even if you do not have complete mastery of the language, grammar, spelling and so on, you can employ an editor, or use an app like **ProWritingAid** to help you with these things. But they cannot create the essential idea for you. They can only clean up, organize, and correct your word structure.

This is the time to accept the fact that you might require a group of people to get your book completed and, at some point, it will be important to consider who you need on the team. First, understand that geographic location means nothing anymore and this will help you find the right people, at the right time, who will work in your best interests. Everything can be done from the comfort of your computer if you deal with book writing coaches, researchers, editors, designers, artists, marketers, printers, distributors, agents and publishers. We will not spend too much time in this book on the area of social networking, marketing, e-books and readers or the various formats needed for these important areas. If you decide to self-publish, you will find a complete library of information on **Amazon-KDP** (the world's largest bookseller). A site like **Draft2Digital** will provide all the information you need to publish on the other retailers, like Barnes and Noble, Kobo, Apple, and many more.

It is important, however, to know that you are responsible, regardless of having a publisher or not, for the marketing of your book. That may come as a surprise to some to learn that landing a publishing contract does not mean the end of your relationship with your book, but the beginning of your job to sell it. It may also come as a surprise to some, if you have not written and published before, that to land that traditional contract, you will most likely have to sign over all the rights to your book including foreign language, movie, audio and most importantly today, the digital rights.

Please be careful and consider all the pros and cons and don't be too eager to give away your hard work too easily. Most of the industry experts have a personal axe to grind and there are very few lawyers, accountants and other objective viewers (unless they have written and released a few of their own titles in this changing period) who have hands-on knowledge of today's world of publishing. The world of book creation is in a total state of change. Staying current, while protecting yourself and making sure that you, as the author, maximize your returns, will take some research and astute business decisions. The best advice I can give you is to consider the motivations of the person who is offering you advice and be sure that it is really advice and not a sales pitch.

This book has covered some very important areas that relate to "Know-How" already, but they bear repeating and review and I encourage you to do so. We have discussed some ways to create an "expert status" for yourself by reading current information on your topic in blogs and other online locations and through reading the top 3 books in your topic. We have covered the 7 characteristics of a bestselling title, and you should have a good, if not completed, working title by now. We have mentioned the importance of creating a time and place for your daily writing. I suppose a coffee shop will work for this purpose. Some very successful writers have started out that way, like J. K. Rowling, the author of the Harry Potter series. She seemed to make it work. Even I, your humble servant, wrote my first two books in the food court of a shopping mall. I am a strong believer in the idea of having an outline for each section with you (the map boards) but if you are creating a place outside your home office, you could always bring it with you in your notebook and then replace it with the next one when ready or just keep the whole works in a three-ring binder for easy reference on the go. You can also create your map boards on a couple of different websites and have them available through your internet connection. You will find these services here: www.bubbl.us and www.mindapp.com

We have also touched on the idea of creating a "team" of experts who would be available to take care of the areas of authorship that you do not want to do yourself. While your primary responsibility is to create your manuscript, you could do some of the other jobs yourself or contract them out. In the conventional world of publishing, the publisher undertakes some of these responsibilities, like editing and design. They usually also have control over title and cover creation besides distribution channels and so forth. If you decide to turn over these areas to a conventional publisher, then you really only need to turn your thoughts to promotion. If you are going to keep control of your book, then you also need to accept responsibility for the other parts of making it available in a professional format to your readers. This brings us to editing.

Chapter 17

EDITING

According to reedsy.com, there are several types of editing, and each is very important to producing a professional quality book.

EDITORIAL ASSESSMENT

An initial overall assessment of your book is done in broad strokes with little actual rewriting.

SUBSTANTIVE EDITING

A much more detailed analysis of the big picture qualities of your work and any inconsistencies. You will usually get a copy of your manuscript returned with changes suggested and defined.

COPY EDITING

Spelling, grammar, run-on sentences, repetitive words, capitalization and my personal favorite, passive voice.

PROOF READING

The last stage before printing or uploading your files and the last chance to make any corrections before the world gets to offer their criticism.

Have I said that everyone needs an independent editor? Can I say it again... and again...? We all need a fresh set of eyes on our work, period! Choose editors with care but, without exception, choose an editor. There are several professional editor organizations found online and most times they have a method of entering criteria that will help you choose the right one for your work. Some criteria you might wish to consider will include experience and educational levels, their own website information, references, familiarity with your topic, and so on. A few words of caution here are necessary; everything that we thought we knew about the book process is changing, including the reader, and you may need an editor who understands this. The language itself is constantly morphing and this might be important to your reader depending on your topic. There used to be hard and fast rules of grammar, punctuation and spelling and some might feel as though they are under attack, but really, they are simply evolving. If a generation raised on YouTube, TikTok, Instagram, and Facebook reads your book, there is not much point in insisting on the proper usage of the King's English - you will lose all credibility with your audience. Likewise, there is a very real move towards authenticity, not necessarily by writers, but readers, and they demand the same in their books. This means that it is perfectly alright to write similarly. Your editor needs to know that is how you want to proceed. You will need to have a conversation with an editor that explains all this while still trusting her to make sure your information flows and connects properly. You can set yourself apart from other writers by insisting that you maintain correct, but up-to-date style and technical aspects without constricting your connection to the reader. Once again, know your reader!

A tip for interviewing a prospective editor: ask them what "style guide" they prefer to use. If they do not know what you are talking about, run! If they name an acceptable style guide, such as Chicago or Oxford, (there are others) you will at least have the comfort of knowing that they have some understanding of what editing is. You should Google "writing style guides," with the quotation marks, to familiarize yourself with this important part of the professional editor's arsenal. That, combined with checking references and background, should provide a good start. The spell and grammar check in Word in not enough, assuming that you want to set yourself apart from the over-hyped marketing gibberish available both online and in some very low-quality e-books and vanity press "publications."

Technology is changing everything at a pace that is hard to comprehend. We need to consider some applications that will allow an author to approach editing in a new light. Copy editing can be done with the help of a program like **ProWritingAid** and others, and **Microsoft Word** continues to improve their suggestions. Artificial Intelligence is transforming our approach to almost everything, including writing and editing. Some people are still painting AI as a bogey man straight out of a B-grade horror movie. But change challenges most of us and then we end up accepting it as normal. Steve Jobs was asked, who would ever want or need a computer in their home? Hmmmm!

You might have a more formal speaking approach and you want your writing to reflect who you really are. If you write in one style and speak in a different style, there is a disconnect from your audience. To reflect an air of authenticity, one that is real, it will be necessary to allow your writing to mimic your speaking. Speaking of speech, let's consider this idea: if you were making a platform speech (and if your book works, you might) would you say it the same way? In that vein, would you use profanity, humor, poetry, and so on? If you would not use a word in front of a live audience, don't use it in your book. In terms of profanity, less is more. We have become immune to swearing (once again, depending on WHO you are writing to) but, it will be much more powerful when used sparingly in non-fiction writing, although the topic of weight loss might create the need for a few choice and shi#*y words.

If you are creating your book to appeal to a specific personality type (something I highly recommend), then your language, flow, layout, and style will need to appeal to that demographic. Some online research into the Meyer's Briggs or DISC system of personality recognition and what appeals to each will be invaluable in creating this kind of targeted product. Start by learning what your own personality profile is and realize that you will naturally write to your own type and then decide if you wish to spread your wings.

A few things to keep in mind as you create your book:

- what technology is necessary to create and deliver your book

- keep a paper and pen beside your bed and in your pocket

- write your own quotes and sound bites

- be alert to stories, illustrations, charts, questions and sidebars

- find someone to keep you accountable for daily writing

- create a consistent time and space

- create a list of team members and their job descriptions

Who might you need to have on your team to make this book a reality?

- Coach/Mentor to keep you on track, focused,

accountable, encouraged, on purpose, confident, organized. This person should be experienced, objective, and knowledgeable and have only your best interests in mind. They need to be both a taskmaster and a cheerleader

- editor - check references and experience - consider referrals

- cover designer - be sure you have several choices or create and evaluate several possibilities from a DIY site like **BookBrush**

- layout designer - not always necessary for e-book formatting or get an app called **Atticus**

- marketing person who is familiar with the book industry and new media

- publicist

- agent

- publisher

- printer

- distributor

This is not a complete list and many times you will do some of this work yourself and may not need several of the services, but insist on an independent editor please.

There are incredible advances in technology that allow you to verbally create a book, too. Software that will allow you to speak and then have your computer translate that into the written word. For professional speakers, this may be a great way to create a rough written copy of your speeches to include in a book. It is interesting that these forms of software are not only improving but becoming more acceptable in schools as ways to write reports. Monitor this area, since the quill and parchment may not be the only option for creating your masterpiece. Speaking of editing, it is interesting to note that even top level bestsellers by highly successful authors often have the occasional typo in their final editions.

Chapter 18

BOOK BUSINESS

I'm not sure that poverty comes with any special privileges, blessings or acknowledgements, even for authors and artists. Living in obscurity in a dark basement suite in your parent's home while you labor on your manuscript in the vague hope that "if you write it, they will read it," is the stuff of B movies. An author, in today's world, can be well paid for her work, but she must take responsibility for the business side of her writing life. An author was always responsible for the business side of writing, but for many years they have hidden behind agents, publishers and retailers and could use them as an excuse. The publishing house was blamed for not paying enough attention to the author, or not promoting them, or assigning enough marketing funds, etc. etc.

For a long time, that excuse was fairly plausible given the delivery systems for books and the high cost of marketing and promotion, but all of that has changed with the internet and most importantly, social networking. Attempting to give you a definitive marketing plan around these two phenomena is beyond the purview of this book, but let's take a quick look at some things that are absolute musts:

- promotion plan - you can never begin this process too early and you will have to create an organized approach to letting people know that you and your book exist

- 15 second pitch - start with creating an "elevator pitch" which is like the answer to the question, **"What's your book about?"** Imagine getting on an elevator unexpectedly with someone you recognize who asks what you are doing, and you answer, "Writing a book." The next question out of their mouth is, "What's it about?" and your answer is absolutely critical; so critical that I recommend you craft it and practice it. It is called an elevator pitch because you imagine you complete your answer in the time to get on and off an elevator - 15 seconds is the average. Do not anticipate and answer all of their questions, but leave room for them to want more. You will find help for this on the internet if you search "elevator pitch" with the surrounding quotations. According to Entrepreneur magazine, a good elevator pitch has 3 elements, 1. Stimulate interest, 2. Transition that interest, 3. Share a vision.

- a website - this seems obvious, but it is essential for an author. The first page should clearly and simply state who you are and what you write about since most visitors will never get beyond this page and they will not search for the information, so make it obvious and easy. You can lead them to a page that tells more about your book or books and include a shopping cart so they can buy it immediately or at least a link to where they can purchase immediately, like Amazon.

- a blog allows you to build a following, update frequently and market occasionally. Some suggestions; post at least twice a week, keep its tone friendly, include your picture, don't overload it with sales pitches; this is your chance to create a relationship with your readers and offer value for your reader's time. You can find volumes of information on how to set up and market blogs on their hosting sites and elsewhere. Two of the biggest blog formats are Blogger and WordPress. Start with a visit to their sites and watch and follow other people's blogs to learn how and what to do. And one last word of advice specifically for writers: we have a tendency to create blogs that are too long - keep it around 500 words for maximum impact.

- Ezine and other online magazines. We discussed earlier how to create and become an expert in the field you wish to write about. In that process, you will definitely run across Ezine, Hub, Squidoo and many other online magazine formats. Once you feel comfortable with your topic, join these various magazines as a contributing author and submit articles on your topic. Each one has slightly different criteria for submitting to their platform, but this will help to build an audience. In every case, you will have the opportunity at the end of your article to identify yourself and include a link to your website or blog. Eventually, you will start getting picked up by other sites and quoted, thus creating a base for your expertise and a market for your book. These sites rarely allow blatant commercial pitches for your book, but if you show your expertise and your ability to write, you will drag a portion of the readers to your own site.

- one-pager is simply that, an outline of your book on one page. There are various formats and techniques for doing this and you should consider things like colors, pictures, drawings and the amount of white space. You might think of the posters that are used to market movies and see if you can learn from them how to market your book. The one-pager must be available for printing so that you can use it at any speaking or networking opportunities, digitally as a PDF so that you can send it out to subscribers, contacts, reviewers and so on. I would suggest creating a very well thought out design and then having a professional graphic designer actually prepare it in various formats for your use. If you are a DIYer, look at **BookBrush**.

- social media marketing is a big subject and there are thousands of self-appointed experts out there who will gladly take your money and promise amazing results. I think it is as much art as science and luck as planning, but at the very minimum, you need to take an active role here. Your topic will drive you to the media that will be best, but if your book is related to a business subject, then LinkedIn is a must. Actually, it is not so much the topic as it is the ideal reader that we have already discussed - where do they hang out online? At this time, Facebook, TikTok, Instagram, and Twitter/X must be very high on your list of social networking places to have a presence. Frankly, these are the big ones right now and I would spend 80% of my "social networking" time there and then go after smaller fish if possible. One word of caution:

many people think they can hire someone "to do" social networking for them - you can't. You can spend your money hiring someone, but they cannot duplicate your words and thoughts. You need to create the time to do this yourself, notwithstanding that you might contract someone to show you how.

- marketing platform is a term to describe your own direct contacts who have given you per-mission to send them information. This is a valuable list that a non-fiction writer needs to be constantly cultivating through captur-ing names and email addresses from sub-scribers to his blog or website or through any other means that is legal and accept-able. There are several companies that can help you do this and keep you out of the spam folder. Learn about www.**AWeber**.com and www.**MailChimp**.com and begin under-standing what "permission marketing" is all about. This is asking people for permission to send them information that is valuable to them. If you do not have their permission, it is called spam and, in some countries, this is being made illegal. It is not surprising since, as of this time, 294 BILLION e-mail messages are sent per day and 89 percent are spam. You don't want to be part of that. Your direct family and close friends may tolerate a few messages attempting to sell your book, but no one else will.

Let's get something straight right away. Unless absolutely everything in the universe lines up perfectly, you are not likely to become wealthy beyond your wildest dreams with your first book.

There are a significant number of modern authors who will give their book away for free because of the abundance that comes after having a book. What does this mean to us when we are trying to write the best book we can? Where is the value of giving something away for nothing?

The real return is in the ancillary products that can, if you plan for it, result from being the author of a book. Becoming a platform or workshop speaker might be one thing you have already thought of when you began this process. You might already be a speaker, but your book will give you increased authority and, possibly, increased fees along with the exposure. Non-fiction writers can start workshops, coaching, produce workbooks, webinars, teleseminars, blog radio shows, audio books, CD's and exotic group trip/workshops. There are an endless number of possibilities to leverage your book into many other sources of income and opportunity. Combined with a public relations campaign, some creativity and an organized approach, the sky is the limit.

This is an area that should be on your radar, even before you start writing, because it will and should change the way you craft a book. If it leaves your readers wanting more, then your responsibility as an author is to provide more. Today's non-fiction readers want short, entertaining, to-the-point books that address an issue that is important to them, giving them a solution, direction or series of possibilities. This gives you the opportunity to offer more products, books and other things of value to your followers, or your tribe. You also find that you can re-purpose sections of your book to create short blogs, pamphlets, speeches, courses and more.

It is important to mention an area that many early-stage authors may not have thought about, and it influences how you will write your book. There is a very lucrative market for books that are written specifically for non-bookstore markets. These are used as promotional items by companies and organizations who give the book away as a bonus for buying something from them. The genuine beauty of this market is that there are no returns; a sale is a sale, period. If you write a book that aligns with the principles or aspirations of a particular group of people, then look for natural tie-ins and make a presentation. Thousands of books are marketed this way. For instance, you might write a book about retirement planning and connect with a bank or other financial institution that will benefit them, their clients, and you. A book about weight loss has natural tie-ins to nutrition companies, athletic outlets, and organizations that promote health and fitness. I urge you not to dismiss this relationship too quickly; many authors have had incredible success with this type of program. If you start your thinking from a place of creating a win/win/win proposition, you will be on the road to some serious commercial success in this area.

One danger, and opportunity, of writing a non-fiction, how-to book is that information, sources, and technology are moving so quickly that our efforts can become dated overnight. There are many solutions to this issue, like writing another book, revising your current one, and creating a newsletter for your readers.

Chapter 19

OPPORTUNITY

Just how many times does OPPORTUNITY knock? Once, according to some ancient saying, but what do you think? The world is full of opportunities, and they are increasing and magnifying daily. Thinking that only one opportunity exists denies us all the chance to grow, share, experience, improve, and get on with our lives. Often, we pass by opportunities and see others turn negative and so on, but that simply makes us better authors. I really mean that the experiences in our lives, especially the challeng-ing ones, are what we have to share with the world and give us a new opportunity; the opportunity to make a difference and isn't that one reason you wrote a book and also why you are still reading this one?

New authors often worry about the possibility that they have nothing unique to add, that it has all been said before, but that simply is not true. You have a unique set of life experiences, a unique way of saying things, and every one of your readers will hear it differently. In the how-to/self-help genre, this combination of circumstances creates a series of possibilities to make a real difference in an infinite number of different ways. Your uniqueness makes it possible for you to add great value to the conversation, and your book is the basic vehicle for making that happen.

We covered the idea of what your book is about earlier and touched upon your motivations for writing the book. But as you work your way through some of the organizational things, it is good to refocus on why you are doing this. Authoring a book brings instant credibility - I'm not sure that is completely justified, but it is completely accurate. If you are trying to set yourself apart in your field of endeavor (your day job), climb the ladder of success in a company or industry, even land a new or better job, a book will give you credentials that nothing else can. A physical book, printed, bound and

professional, is the greatest calling card of all because it establishes your credentials on a topic like
nothing else. Blogs, websites, public speaking, even
newspaper columns don't carry the same cache as
a physical book.

Something else happens when a box full of your
own books arrives at your home and it is a sense
of self-worth, confidence, and positive energy that
flows around you. This positive energy attracts people, and they treat you with a newfound respect.
You are one of the very few people, out of the millions, who say that they want to write a book that
actually have. This brings a series of other opportunities, some of which we have mentioned in the
section on "ancillary products." In a recent conversation with a highly regarded international speaker,
he said that it would have been much easier to
have created his book first and started his speaking
career second. The book would have given him a
platform and a message that would have made his
acceptance as a speaker less difficult. He stated that
it would have made the marketing and booking part
of his job much easier.

As an author, you can re-purpose parts of your book to blogs, ezines and other media, all of which may attract conventional media when they are looking for an expert in the field to interview and quote. This leads to even more opportunities. Even if you decide on the self-publishing route for your first book, the exposure has attracted mainstream publishers, for some authors. You showed several important things to them: your writing ability, your marketing ability, and your building of an audience. These are the things that publishers need in order to offer an author their support. The other old saying, "nothing attracts success like success" is in your power to make true.

Chapter 20

OWNERSHIP

Everything you write is automatically covered under copyright law, without taking any further legal steps. If you didn't know this already, it is unnecessary to run for legal advice and start any sort of proceedings to protect your creative output. It is yours. On very rare occasions, there can be a dispute about something that has huge commercial value; otherwise, there would be no dispute, naturally enough. If you have any reason to be concerned about this, here's what you do. Print out a copy of your completed edited manuscript and put it into a sturdy envelope. Take it to the post office and send it by registered mail to YOURSELF. When it comes in the mail, sign the receipt from the post office and put the **UNOPENED** envelope somewhere safe. If there is ever a legal dispute, you can present your unopened and dated (the postmark) envelope and manuscript forward to the courts, through your legal counsel, for verification of you as its author. This will establish copyright and ownership of your work and is acceptable in most lawful jurisdictions. This assumes that what you have written is original and not copied from somewhere else without acknowledgement.

In addition, you automatically own all the other rights to your work, including digital, audio, foreign language, distribution, movie and anything else you can think of, or that might become available in the future. This is accurate UNLESS you have sold them to someone else. If you are negotiating anything regarding your book, read the contract yourself besides having legal counsel, because the family friend who is also a real estate lawyer may not understand this industry as well as you need to.

Let's also discuss ISBNs and I realize that most readers who are writers will be familiar with this term and what it is. This is a unique identifying code number that is attached to every book and every distinct version of the book. That means that if you publish a hard copy edition of your book, it will have one ISBN and then, if you also create an e-book version, it will have another number to identify it separately. If you sell the rights to your book to another party, like a publisher, they will get the ISBN and you don't need to bother with it. Many self-publishing companies, e-book publishers and various consulting outfits will offer to get the ISBN for you. My advice to clients is to keep control of the ISBN themselves - it really is not an onerous task to get one. Here are the websites for the Canadian, UK and U.S. sites that provide them - set up an account and you find that when you need another one, it is even easier.

Canada   http://www.collectionscanada.gc.ca/

U.S.   http://www.isbn.org/standards/home/index.asp

UK   www.isbn.nielsenbookdata.co.uk

You can search ISBN for any other country of residence and find this information too, but be careful about paying agencies for services that can be provided directly to you from the governing body. This will ensure that all the correct information regarding the publisher, reordering, pricing and so on remains in your hands, where it belongs. Just a note,

Amazon/KDP and other digital platforms will offer to provide an ISBN, but I would seriously advise that you get your own. And also, a company that simply prints your book on your instructions is not the publisher. You are, until or unless, you have sold those rights and received compensation for them.

Chapter 21

COMPLETE

That brings us to the end of your book - when does that happen, you ask? I have talked with two distinct groups about this topic: the group who would keep writing forever until someone says, "Enough, stop already!" and the group who reaches the end of their patience and would prefer to hand it over and never see it again. A few facts to consider, as they pertain to non-fiction books:

- there are no rules regarding "ideal" book length

- shorter is definitely more popular today

- nothing wrong with creating a second book

- if you create an e-book only, people will print out up to 100 pages on their own printer

- for hard copy books, you can change sizes and fonts to adjust the number of pages

- e-readers can change their own font sizes

We should include a few final thoughts about marketing, but keep in mind that this subject is changing every day and can never really be complete. If you are self-publishing, there are several printing services available at this time and the number of copies you expect to sell personally will determine who to use. For instance, if you are absolutely certain that you will sell over 1000 copies, then opt for an offset printer where the price per copy will be your lowest. Another option, if you expect your sales to be less than 1000, will be a digital printer where your pricing will be best without the commitment to large inventories gathering dust in your basement. Another service is available and if you set your books up on Amazon and other sites like it, Print-on-Demand (POD) is the highest "per copy" price but does not require the stockpiling of inventory and attempting to guess forthcoming sales. This is the easiest way for early stage authors to handle paperback books as the customer decides how many and pays directly for their copies. You will receive a royalty for each copy sold. There is a significant body of evidence to suggest that retail stores will soon be dedicated to printing on demand while you wait, thus avoiding the need for any shelf space and providing yet another opportunity to hang out and have a latte. This may come to fruition much sooner than most expect.

In addition, if you have decided to self-publish and still want to see your book appear in bricks and mortar bookstores, there are book distributors who have a sales force that call on stores, chains and other outlets. They will take your book on consignment, as do the retailers, and send you payments when the books sell. Keep in mind that you will still be responsible for all advertising, marketing, returns and shipping. As always, read your contract carefully.

Bookstore signings are a great way to spend an afternoon with very low sales potential, unless you can create a bit of enthusiasm among friends and family to come out and support you. For the relatively unknown in the book world, it is a waste of time and money. We often see big name authors make the famous book tour and see them on the news, in the newspapers, being interviewed on the radio, line ups at bookstores and so on. You might well be in that category, but if you are like the other 90%, then only a major publisher can afford to commit the resources to this effort. They will almost never do so for a relative unknown - no matter how well written your book.

Here is an interesting reality check: there are hundreds of thousands of books written every year and the average one that makes it to a store sells 40 copies! You can change that number drastically by keeping the end in mind - from the beginning. Take the selling of your book seriously and search out all available opportunities to tell people about your efforts. Practice your answer to "**What's your book about?**" Be proud of your accomplishment and remember that, of every one hundred people you meet, ninety of them want to write a book, too. And of those ninety, only 1 or 2 will actually complete a book. Congratulations, you are in very exclusive company!

Chapter 22

AFTERWORD

We live in an amazing world on almost every level imaginable. Creating and offering books in this world is every bit as "amazing" as anything else. Everything we thought we knew about authorship is changing before our very eyes. We are witnessing a tsunami of new possibilities in everything from researching, the writing process itself, to the delivery and reading methods. Will books on paper disappear with digital book programs? I doubt it - some things, like photo books, recipe and travel books, and others lend themselves to the traditional production procedures that we expect. Limitations that authors have dealt with in the past, however, are changing, if not disappearing. It is an exciting time to want to write your own book because the possibilities of finding an audience, in numbers that are manageable, profitable and grow-able, have never been better. Everything from traditional hard cover books in traditional bookstores to trade paperbacks, audio books and a wide variety of digital platforms and formats are now directly available to the aspiring author. The excuses for not writing the book of your dreams have to change too, since we cannot blame the office-bound, overworked submissions editor in a publishing conglomerate for not recognizing your inner genius and offering a six-figure publishing contract.

Using the advice and ideas in this book also eliminates the most popular excuse, "... not enough time." One hour a day will produce your book. I know because I have done it several times and I know lots of others, with full-time careers and commitments, who have done the same.

One of my favorite lines from presentations and workshops that I give is that the only real prerequisite for being an author is to first, be a reader and my other favorite line is, "We now stand on the threshold of the golden age of writing." I firmly believe in the truth of both statements. You do too, or you would not have spent the time reading to the end, nor would you believe in the possibility of writing your own book. What is left to do - go back and complete the assignments, field trips and planning and then decide when the hour per day will take place? Yes, it requires discipline, but you already have everything else. If you need someone to hold you accountable for accomplishing your own dream, then enlist someone, but don't wait any longer because when all is said and done, you can have one of two things - reasons, or results. You now get to choose.

If you have found this book useful, please go back to where you bought it and provide a brief review. This is how I, and soon, you can help attract more readers.

w w w . R o b e r t j B a n n o n . c o m

Chapter 23

BIBLIOGRAPHY

ALL MARKETERS ARE LIARS

Seth Godin

Penguin Books   ISBN 1-59184-100-3

THE 4 – HOUR WORK WEEK

Timothy Ferriss

Crown Publishers ISBN 978-0-307-46535-1

WRITE STARTS

Hal Zina Bennett

New World Library ISBN 978-1-57731-689-3

THE COMPLETE ARTIST'S WAY

Julia Cameron

Penguin Group ISBN 978-1-58542-630-0

Dozens of blogs, websites, online courses, and newsletters including:

There is more information than any one person could digest available online, and I encourage you to find sources that appeal to you and follow them.

About the Author

Robert J Bannon is still trying to define what retirement is and how to live it. Leveraging his life as an entrepreneur, sales manager, stockbroker and VP investor relations, along with 10 years as a tax consultant, Bob has written a 6 book series, EXTRA RETIREMENT INCOME IS SEXY, to help retirees create additional income and fulfillment in their life. He has also authored several other non-fiction titles, some of which are included below.

He and his wife live in the foothills of the Rockies and have 2 adult children and 3 grandsons. He continues to travel the world, play golf, and write, balanced with grocery shopping, cooking, and afternoon naps. You can reach him through his website at RobertJBannon.com.

Also By Robert J Bannon

EXTRA RETIREMENT INCOME IS SEXY
Ignite Your Financial Passion and Live the
Lifestyle You Love
BOOK 1
Paperback ISBN 978-0-9739646-9-1
Ebook ISBN 978-1-7382603-0-0

THE PROSPEROUS PEN
Mastering Freelance Writing for Retirement
Riches
Book 2
Paperback ISBN 978-1-7382603-1-7
Ebook ISBN 978-1-7382603-2-4

DIGITAL CLASSROOMS

Unlocking Retirement Riches as an Online Tutor

Book 3

Paperback ISBN 978-1-7382603-3-1

Ebook ISBN 978-1-7382603-4-8

SILVER HAIRED SAGE

Retirees Become Amazing Virtual Assistants & Increase Their Own Income

Book 4

Paperback ISBN 978-1-7382603-5-5

Ebook ISBN 978-1-7382603-6-2

DESIGNING WEALTH

A Retiree's Guide to More Income and Creative Fulfillment

Book 5

Paperback ISBN 978-1-7382603-7-9

Ebook ISBN 978-1-7382603-8-6

GOLDEN INSIGHTS

Unlocking Extra Income – A Retiree's Guide to Surveys & Reviews

Book 6

Paperback ISBN 978-1-7382603-9-3

Ebook ISBN   978-1-7382622-0-5

EASY STOCK MARKET STARTER COURSE
ASIN B09NCFC2FF   ISBN 979-8783059315

THE WEST COAST TRAIL: One Step at a Time
ASIN 172789703X   ISBN 978-1727897036

HOW TO WRITE A BOOK ABOUT WEIGHT LOSS
Or any other non-fiction topic
ISBN PAPERBACK 978-1-7382622-1-2
ISBN E-BOOK   978-1-7382622-2-9

By Lonewolf Notes/RJB
ETSY SHOP MANAGER
ASIN B083XW6CXJ   ISBN 979-8601305228

MY WINE TASTING JOURNAL & NOTEBOOK
ASIN 1676781633   ISBN 978-1676781639

FINANCIAL PLANNER TEMPLATE
ASIN 1676048227   ISBN 978-1676048220

www.ingramcontent.com/pod-product-compliance
Lightning Source LLC
Chambersburg PA
CBHW050509210326
41521CB00011B/2392